EASY PIANO

BILLIE EILISH WHEN WE ALL FALL ASLEEP, WHERE DO WE GO?

ISBN 978-1-5400-7040-1

Visit Hal Leonard Online at
www.halleonard.com

Contact us:
Hal Leonard
7777 West Bluemound Road
Milwaukee, WI 53213
Email: info@halleonard.com

In Europe, contact:
Hal Leonard Europe Limited
42 Wigmore Street
Marylebone, London, W1U 2RN
Email: info@halleonardeurope.com

In Australia, contact:
Hal Leonard Australia Pty. Ltd.
4 Lentara Court
Cheltenham, Victoria, 3192 Australia
Email: info@halleonard.com.au

BAD GUY

Words and Music by BILLIE EILISH O'CONNELL
and FINNEAS O'CONNELL

White shirt now red: ___ my blood - y nose. Sleep - ing, you're on

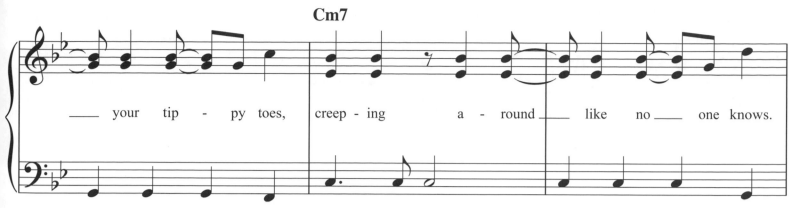

your tip - py toes, creep - ing a - round ___ like no ___ one knows.

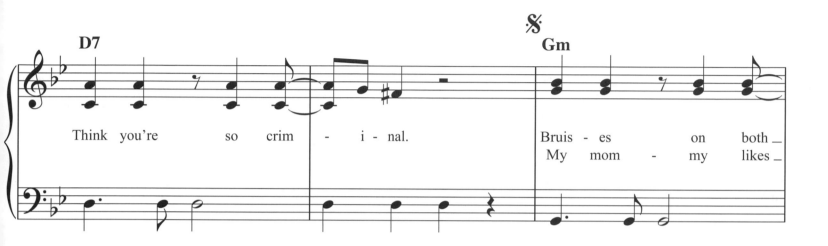

Think you're so crim - i - nal.
Bruis - es on both ___
My mom - my likes ___

___ my knees ___ for you. Don't say thank you ___ or please. ___ I do
___ to sing ___ a - long with me, but she ___ won't sing ___ this song.

what I want, when ___ I'm want - ing to. My soul, so cyn -
If she reads all ___ the lyr - ics, she'll pit - y the men ___

4

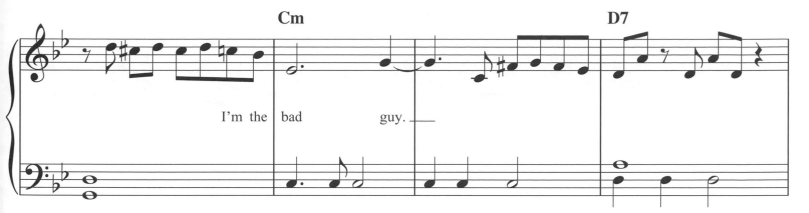

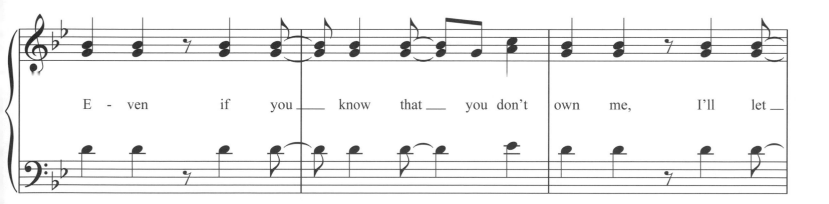

CODA

I'm on - ly good at play - ing bad,

bad.

Slowly

mp

XANNY

Words and Music by BILLIE EILISH O'CONNELL
and FINNEAS O'CONNELL

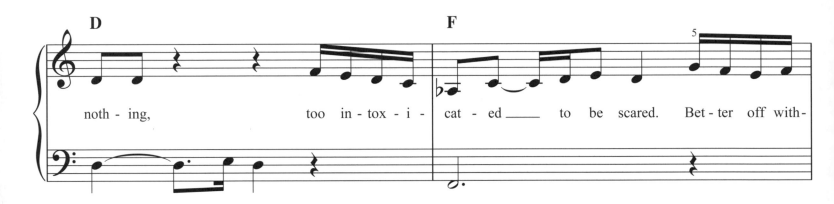

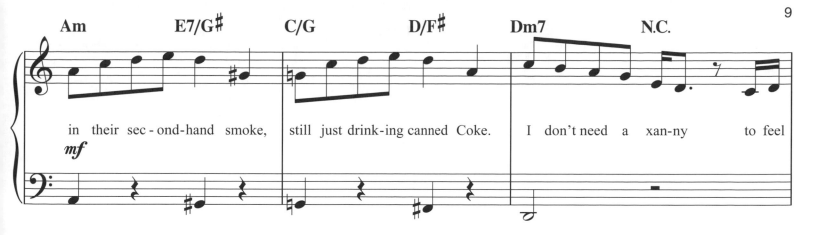

in their sec-ond-hand smoke, still just drink-ing canned Coke. I don't need a xan-ny to feel

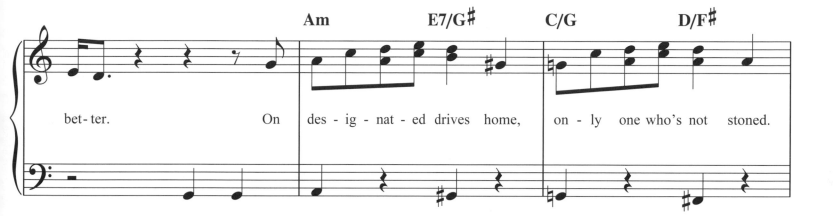

bet-ter. On des-ig-nat-ed drives home, on-ly one who's not stoned.

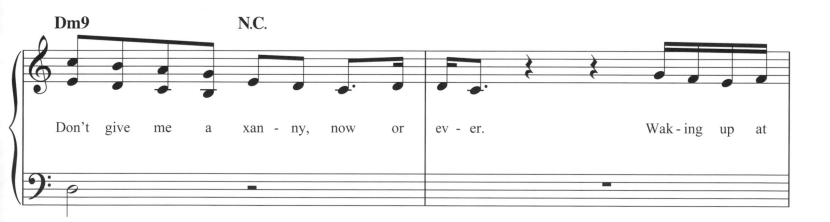

Don't give me a xan-ny, now or ev-er. Wak-ing up at

sun-down, they're late to ev-'ry par-ty. No-bod-y ev-er

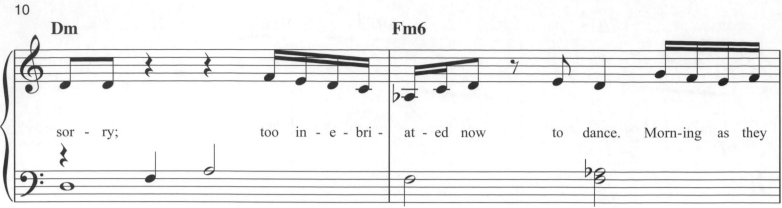

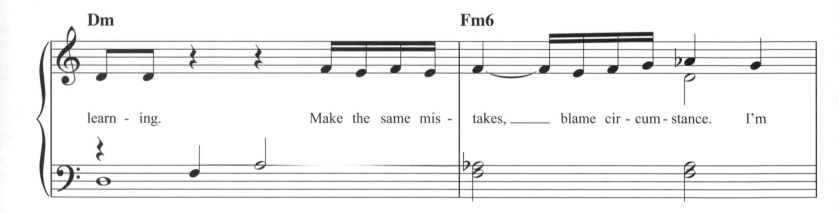

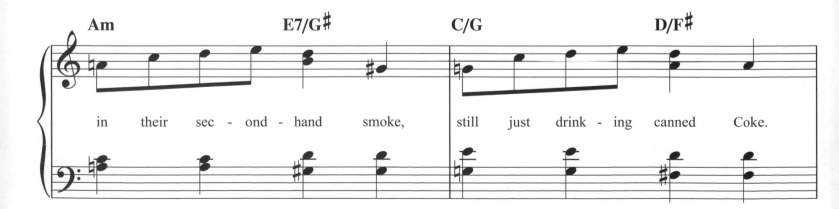

I don't need a xan - ny to feel bet - ter. On

des - ig - nat - ed drives home, on - ly one who's not stoned.

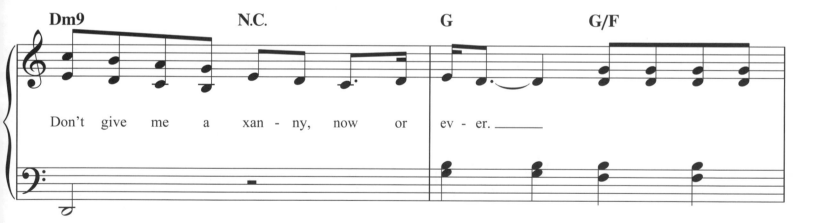

Don't give me a xan - ny, now or ev - er. _____

Please don't try to kiss me on the side - walk on your cig -

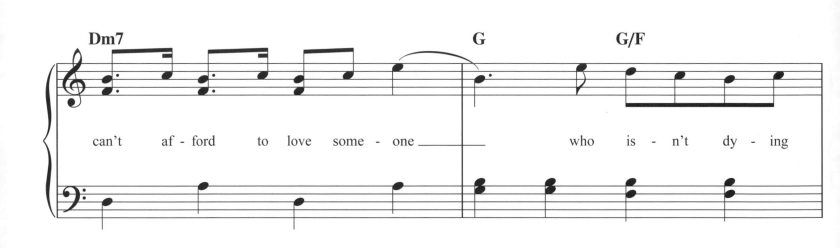

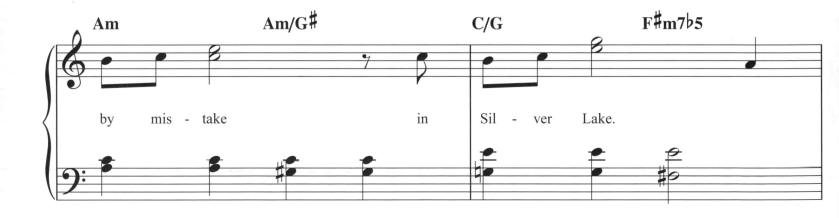

13

bout them? I must be miss-ing some-thing. They just keep do - ing

noth-ing, too in-tox - i- cat-ed to be scared. (Mm, ___

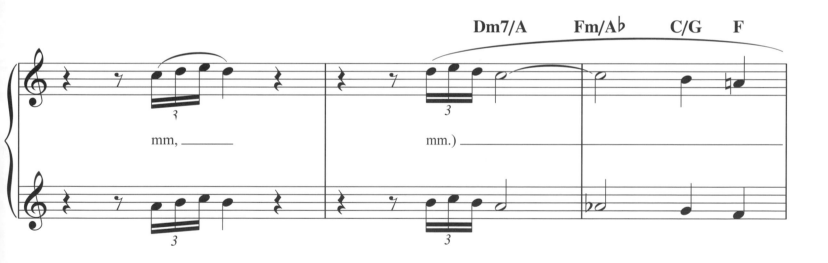

mm, ___ mm.) ___

___ (Come down. Hurt - ing, learn - ing.)

YOU SHOULD SEE ME IN A CROWN

Words and Music by BILLIE EILISH O'CONNELL
and FINNEAS O'CONNELL

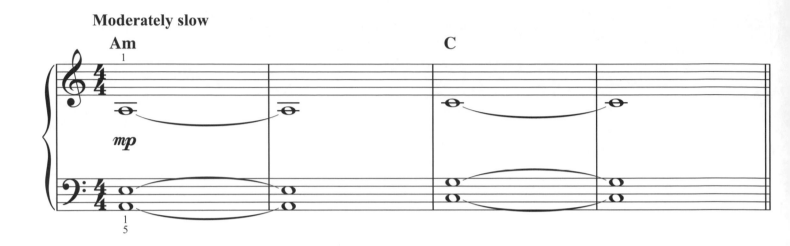

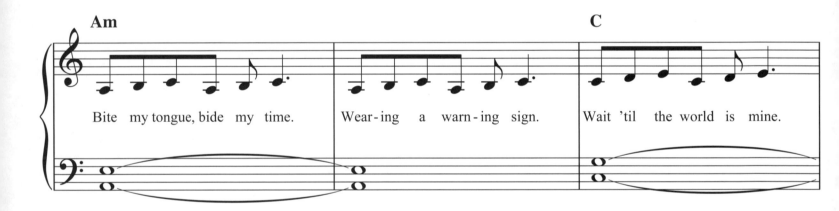

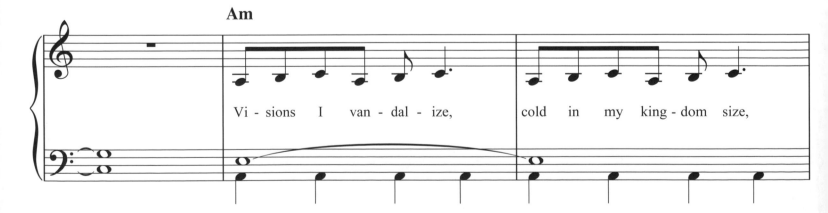

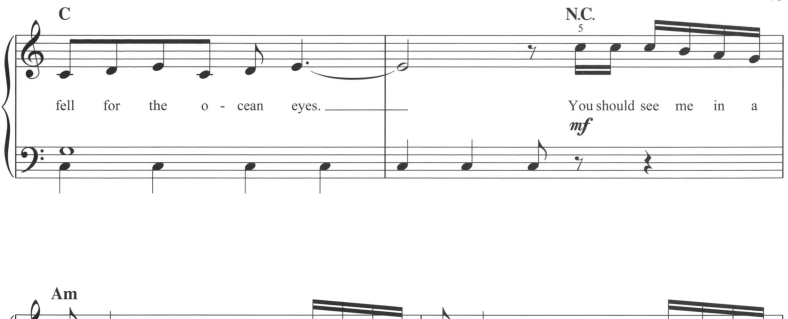

fell for the o - cean eyes. ___ You should see me in a

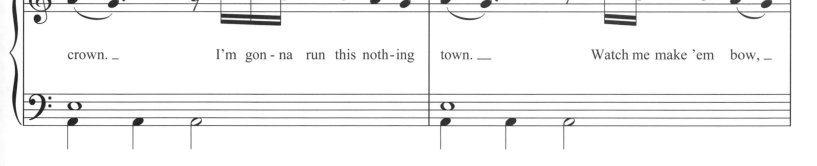

crown. ___ I'm gon - na run this noth - ing town. ___ Watch me make 'em bow, ___

one by, one by one, one by, one by... You should see me in a

crown. ___ Your si - lence is my fa - v'rite sound. ___ Watch me make 'em bow, ___

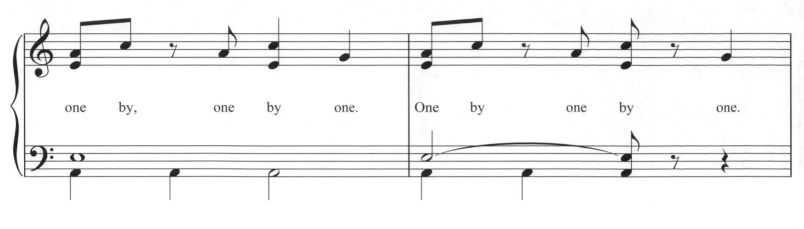

one by, one by one. One by one by one.

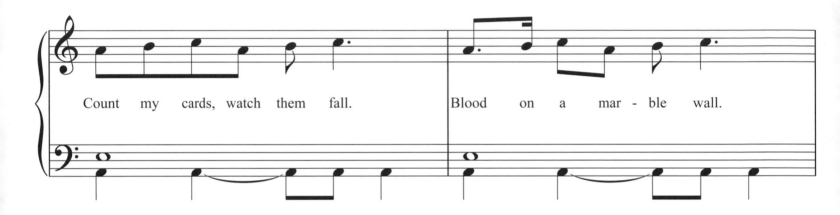

Count my cards, watch them fall. Blood on a mar - ble wall.

C

I like the way they all _____ (scream). _

Am

Tell me which one is worse: liv - ing, or dy - ing first?

Sleep - ing in - side a hearse? _____ (I don't dream.) _____

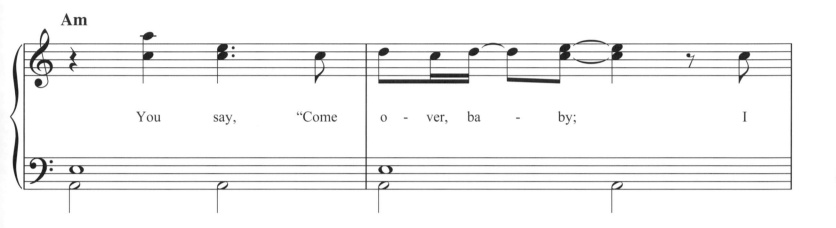

You say, "Come o - ver, ba - by; I

think you're pret - ty." _____ I'm o - kay. I'm

not your ba - by. _____ If you think I'm pret - ty, _____ you should see me in a

ALL THE GOOD GIRLS GO TO HELL

Words and Music by BILLIE EILISH O'CONNELL
and FINNEAS O'CONNELL

My Lu - ci - fer is lone - ly. ____

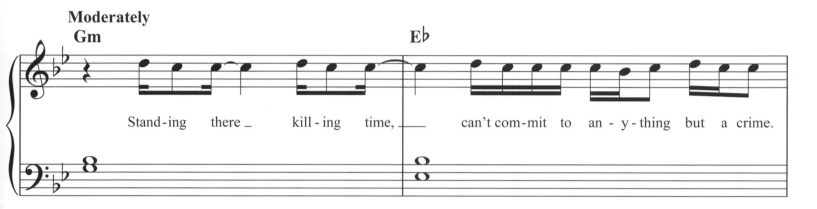

Stand-ing there ____ kill - ing time, ____ can't com-mit to an - y - thing but a crime.

Pe - ter's on va - ca - tion, an o - pen in - vi - ta - tion.

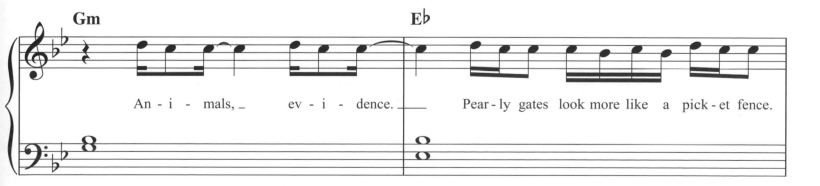

An - i - mals, ____ ev - i - dence. ____ Pear - ly gates look more like a pick - et fence.

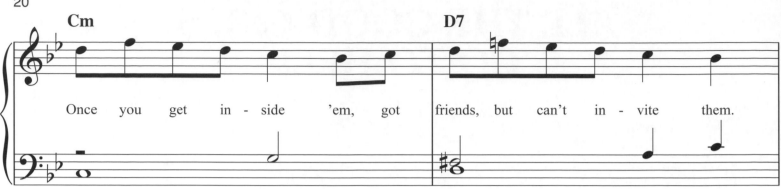

Once you get in - side 'em, got friends, but can't in - vite them.

Hills burn in Cal - i - for - nia. My turn to ig - nore __ you.

Don't say I did - n't warn __ you.

All the good girls go to hell, __ 'cause e - ven God her -

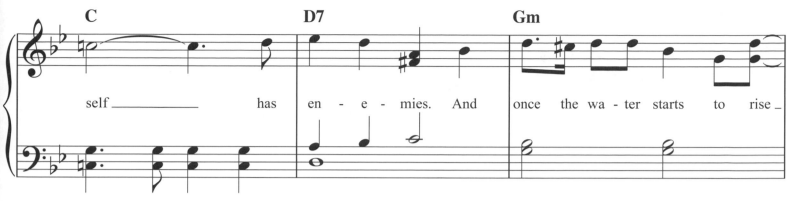

self _____ has en-e-mies. And once the wa-ter starts to rise _

_ and heav-en's out of sight, she'll want the dev-il on her

team. _____ My Lu-ci-fer is lone-ly. _____

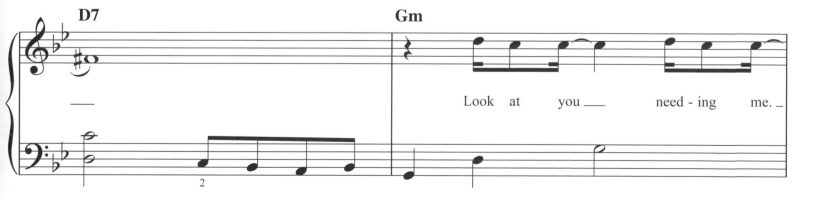

Look at you _ need-ing me. _

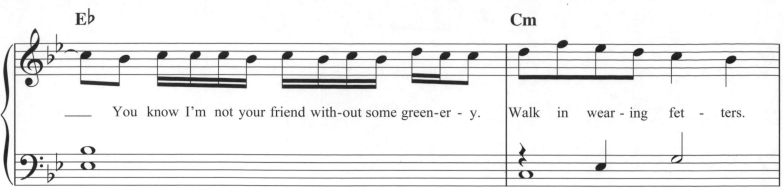

You know I'm not your friend with-out some green-er - y. Walk in wear-ing fet - ters.

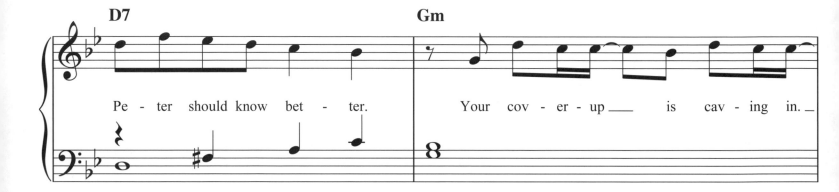

Pe - ter should know bet - ter. Your cov - er - up ___ is cav - ing in. ___

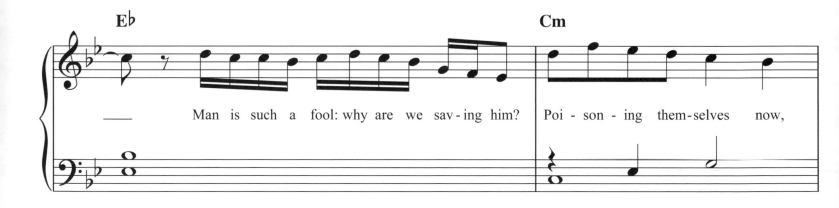

___ Man is such a fool: why are we sav-ing him? Poi - son - ing them-selves now,

beg - ging for our help. Wow.

team. ___ My Lu - ci -

fer is lone - ly. _____ (There's noth - ing left to say _____ now.) _____

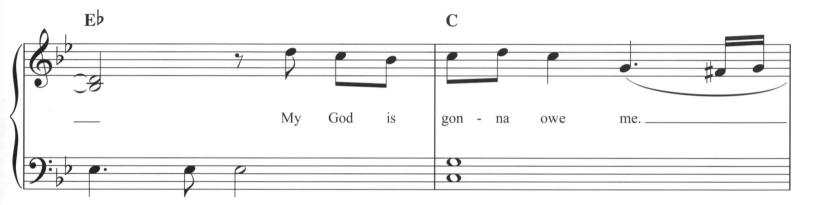

_____ My God is gon - na owe me. _____

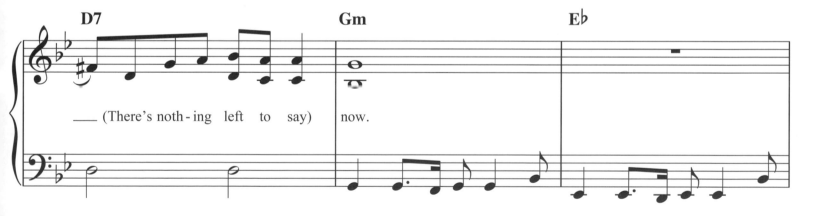

_____ (There's noth - ing left to say) now.

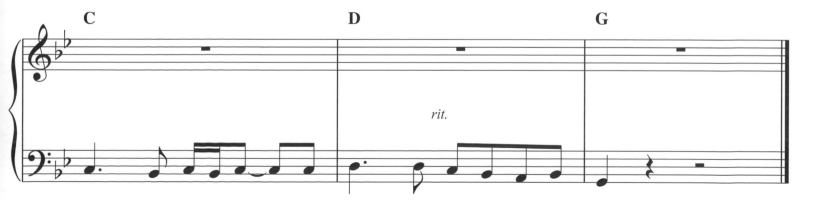

rit.

WISH YOU WERE GAY

Words and Music by BILLIE EILISH O'CONNELL
and FINNEAS O'CONNELL

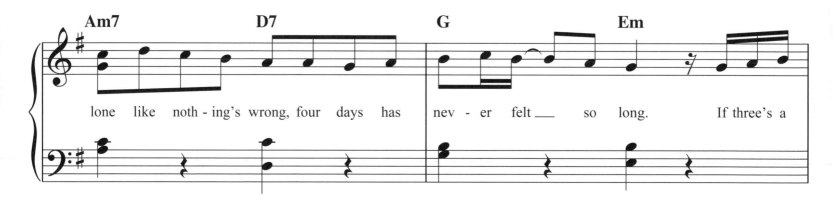

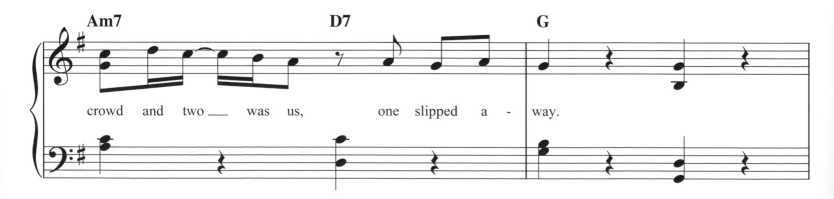

I just wan-na make you feel o - kay, but

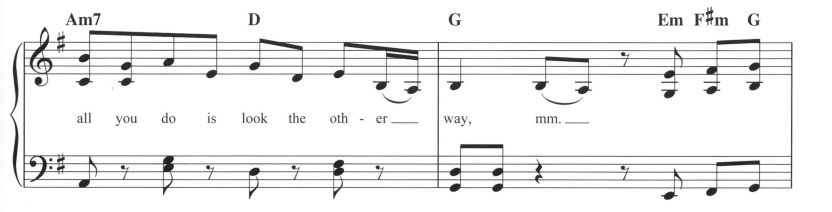

all you do is look the oth - er ____ way, mm. ____

I can't tell you how much I wish I did-n't wan-na stay, ____ mm. ____

I just kind - a wish you were gay. ____ Is there a

rea - son we're not through? Is there a twelve-step just __ for you? Our con-ver-

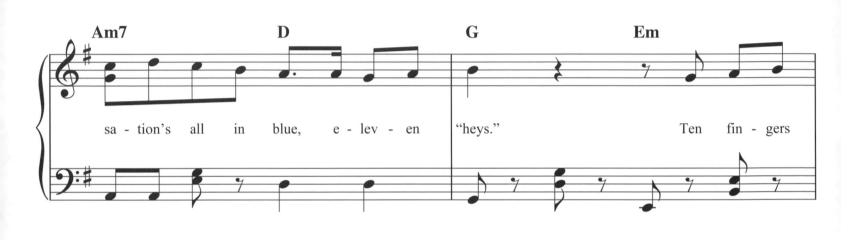

sa - tion's all in blue, e - lev - en "heys." Ten fin - gers

tear - ing out __ my hair, nine times you nev - er made _ it there. I ate a -

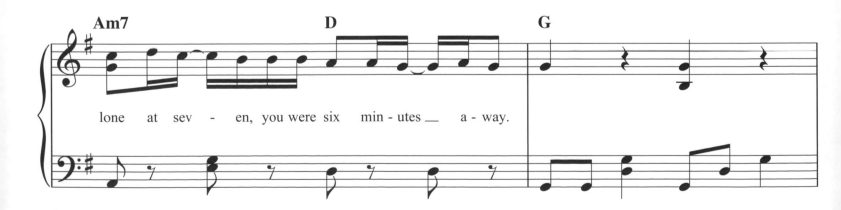

lone at sev - en, you were six min - utes _ a - way.

How'm I s'posed to make you feel o - kay when

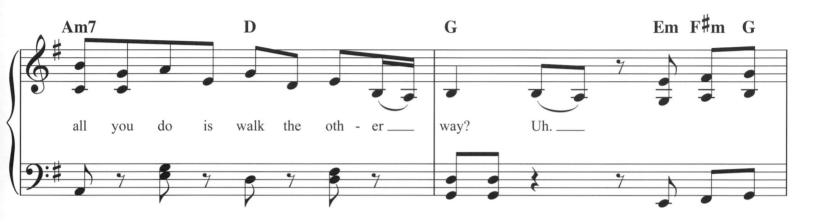

all you do is walk the oth - er ___ way? Uh. ___

I can't tell you how much I wish I did - n't wan - na stay, ___ uh. ___

I just kind - a wish you were gay. ___ To spare my

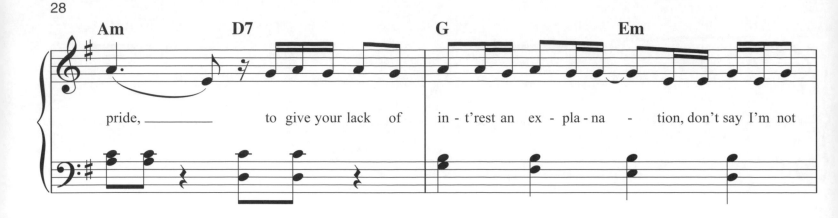

Am   **D7**   **G**   **Em**

pride, _____ to give your lack of in - t'rest an ex - pla - na - tion, don't say I'm not

Am   **D7**   **G**   **Em**

your type.   Just say that I'm not your pre - ferred sex - u - al o - ri - en - ta - tion. I'm so

N.C.   **D7**   **G**   **Em**

self - ish,   but you make me feel help - less, ___ yeah. ___ And I can't

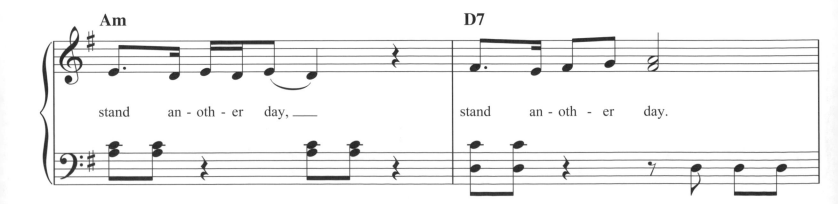

Am   **D7**

stand an - oth - er day, ___ stand an - oth - er day.

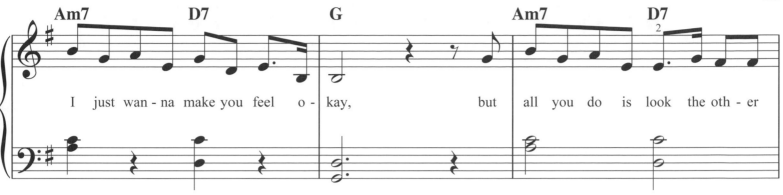

I just wan-na make you feel o - kay, but all you do is look the oth - er

way, mm. I can't tell you how much I wish I did-n't

wan-na stay, mm. I just kind - a wish you were gay.

I just kind - a wish you were gay.

WHEN THE PARTY'S OVER

Words and Music by
FINNEAS O'CONNELL

Gently, with motion

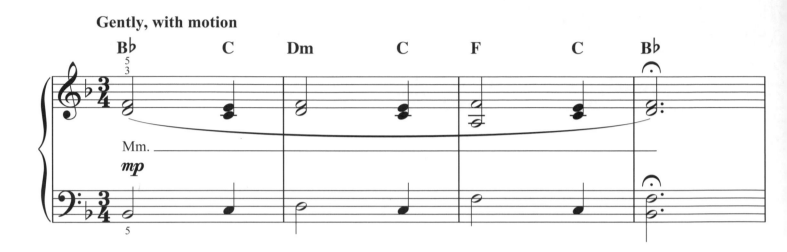

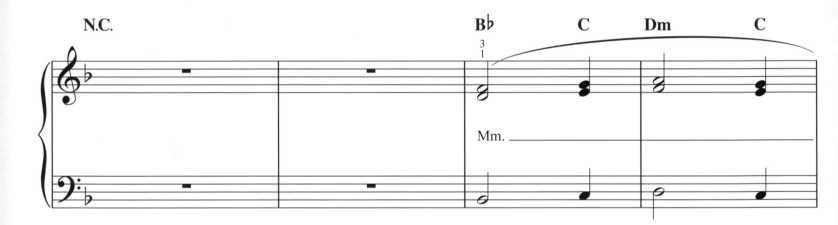

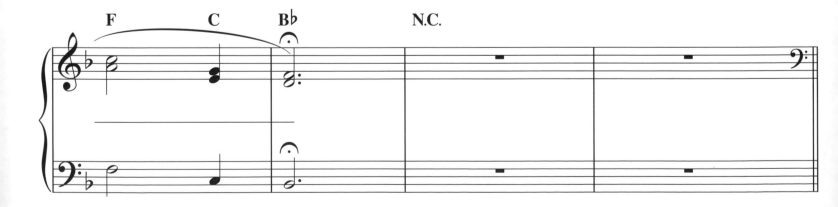

Don't you know I'm no good for you?
Don't you know know too much al - read - y?

I've learned to lose you,
I'll on - ly hurt you

can't af - ford to. ____
if you lct mc. ____

Tore my shirt to stop ____ you bleed - ing.
Call me friend, but keep ____ me clos - er.

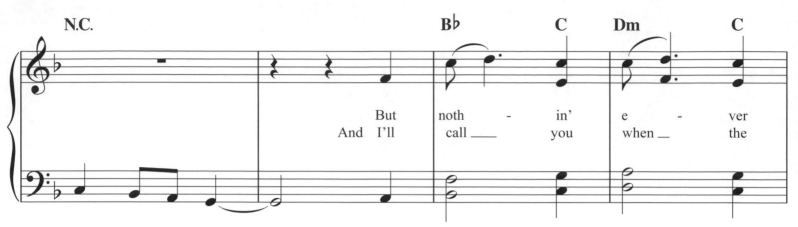

But noth - in' e - ver
And I'll call ____ you when ____ the

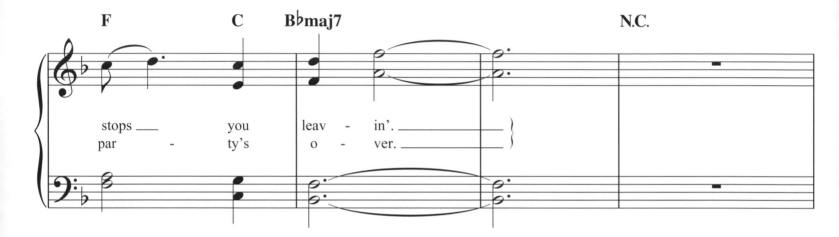

stops ____ you leav - in'. ____
par - ty's o - ver. ____

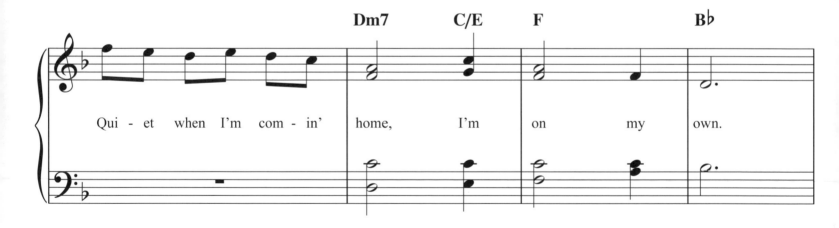

Qui - et when I'm com - in' home, I'm on my own.

I could lie, say I like it like that, like it like that. ____

Bb   **F**   **Gm**   **Dm**   **To Coda** ⊕

I could lie, say I like it like that,

F   **Bb**

like it like that. ____

D.S. al Coda

CODA ⊕

F   **Bb**   **Dm/A**

like it like that. ____ But

Gm   **Dm**   **F**   **Bbmaj9**

noth - in' ____ is bet - ter some - times. ____

Once we've both said our good - byes, _____

___ let's just ___ let ___ it ___ go. ___

___ And let me ___ let you ___ go. ___

Slower

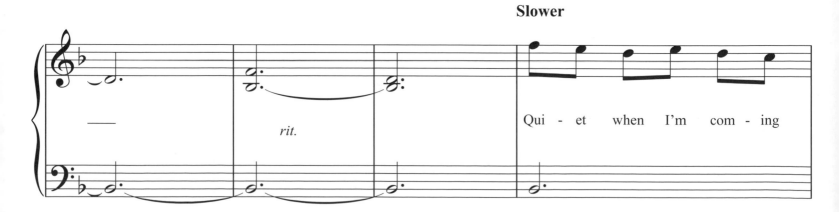

___ *rit.* Qui - et when I'm com - ing

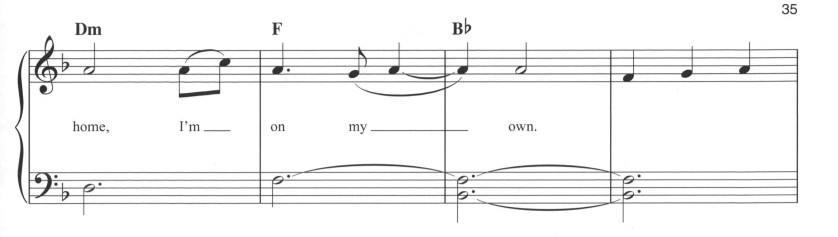

home, I'm ___ on my ___ own.

I could lie, say I like it like that, like it like that. ___

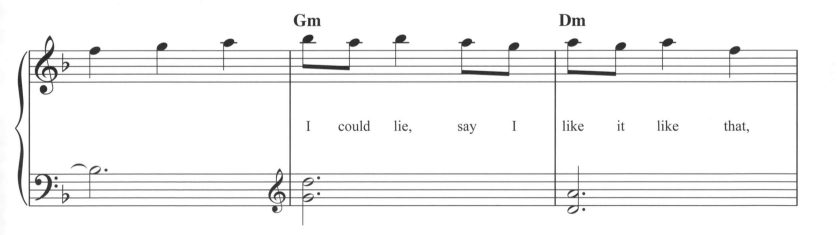

I could lie, say I like it like that,

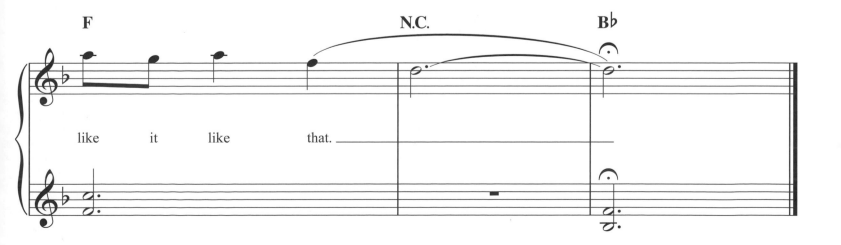

like it like that. ___

8

Words and Music by BILLIE EILISH O'CONNELL
and FINNEAS O'CONNELL

Guess I o - ver - did _____ it, poured my heart out _____ on a chain _____

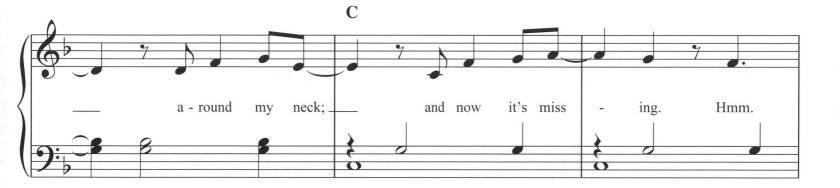

_____ a - round my neck; _____ and now it's miss - ing. Hmm.

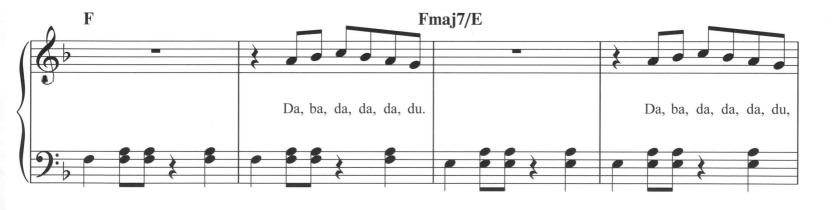

Da, ba, da, da, da, du. Da, ba, da, da, da, du,

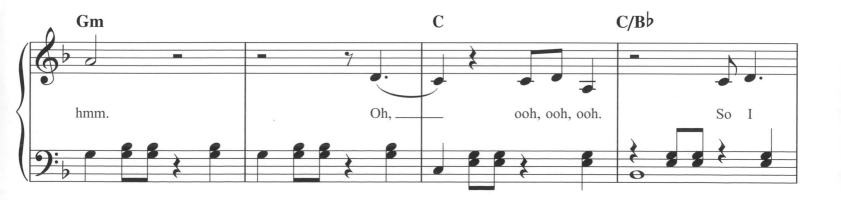

hmm. Oh, _____ ooh, ooh, ooh. So I

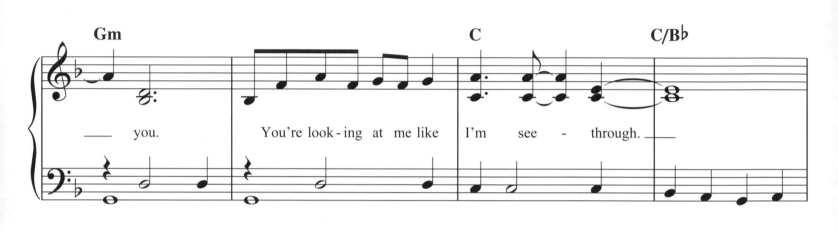

Da, ba, da, da, da, du, dum.

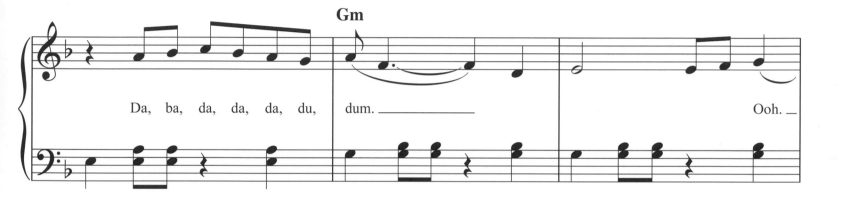

Da, ba, da, da, da, du, dum. _____ Ooh. _

_____ You said, "Don't treat me bad - dly,"

but you said it so sad - ly, _____ so I did the best I

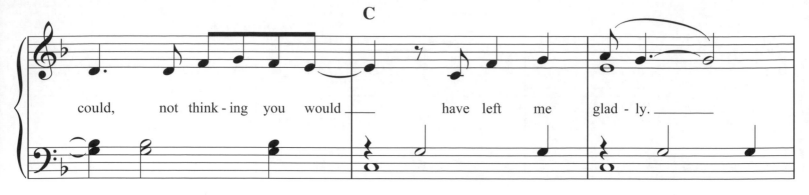

could, not think-ing you would _____ have left me glad - ly. _____

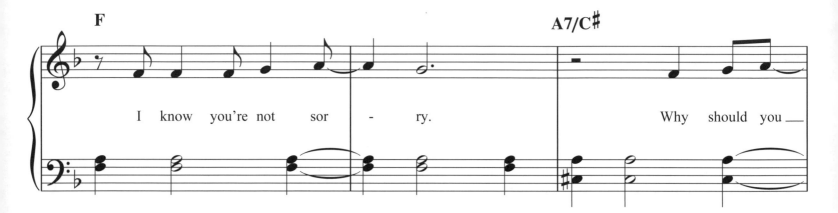

I know you're not sor - ry. Why should you _____

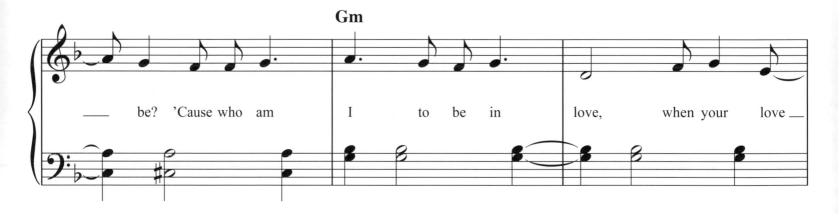

_____ be? 'Cause who am I to be in love, when your love _____

_____ nev - er is for _____ me, me?

Da, ba, da, da, da, du, dum.

Da, ba, da, da, da, du, dum. _____ Ooh. __

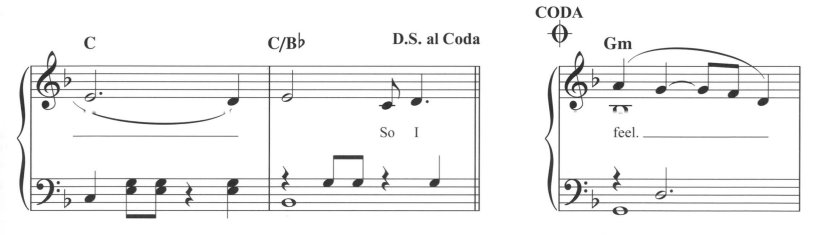

_____ So I feel. _____

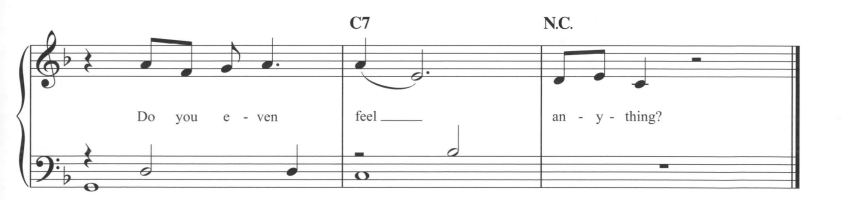

Do you e - ven feel _____ an - y - thing?

MY STRANGE ADDICTION

Words and Music by
FINNEAS O'CONNELL

Moderately

Don't ask ques - tions ____ you don't wan - na know.
Dead - ly fe - ver, ____ please don't ev - er break. Be

Learned my les - son ____ way too long a - go. To be
my re - liev - er, ____ 'cause I don't self-med - i - cate. And it

talk - ing to you, bel - la - don - na, should - 've tak - en a break on an Ox - ford com - ma.
burns like a gin, and I like it. Put your lips on my skin, and I might ig - nite. It

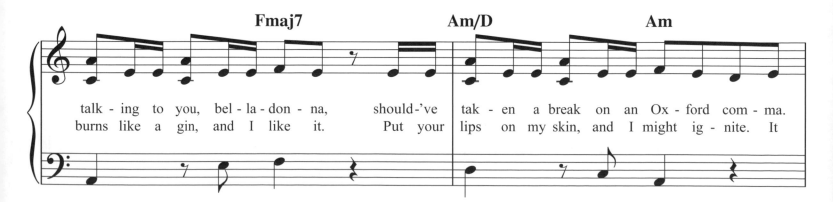

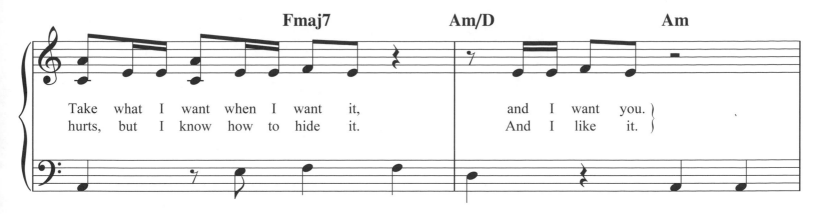

Take what I want when I want it, and I want you.
hurts, but I know how to hide it. And I like it.

Bad, __ bad __ news; one of us is gon-na lose. __ I'm the pow-der, you're the fuse:

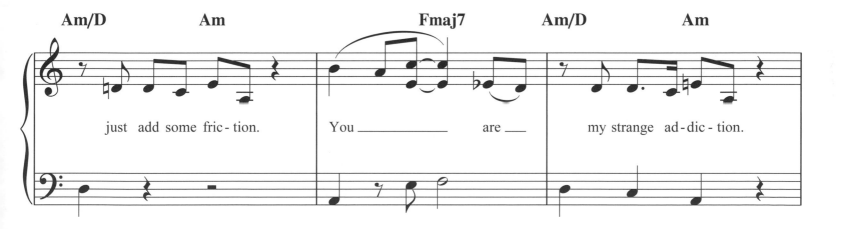

just add some fric-tion. You _____ are __ my strange ad-dic-tion.

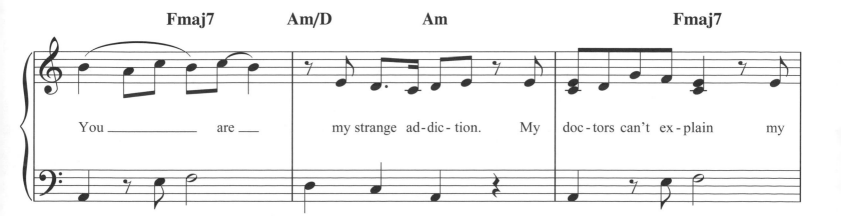

You _____ are __ my strange ad-dic-tion. My doc-tors can't ex-plain my

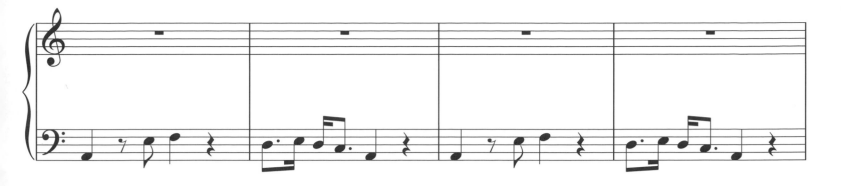

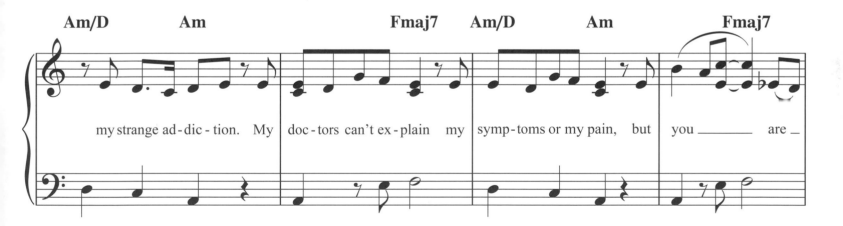

You _____ are _____ my strange ad-dic-tion. You _____ are _____

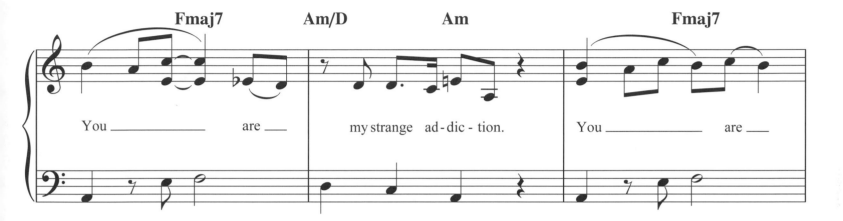

my strange ad-dic-tion. My doc-tors can't ex-plain my symp-toms or my pain, but you _____ are _____

my strange ad-dic-tion.   *"Did you like it? Did you like that?"*   *"Which part?"*

BURY A FRIEND

Words and Music by BILLIE EILISH O'CONNELL
and FINNEAS O'CONNELL

Lyrics: What do you want ___ from me? Why do you run ___ from me?

Lyrics: What are you won - der - ing? What do you know? ___ Why aren't you scared ___ of me?

Why do you care ___ for me? When we all fall ___ a-sleep, where do we go? ___

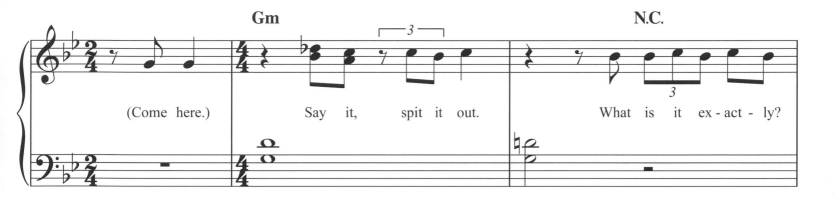

(Come here.) Say it, spit it out. What is it ex-act-ly?

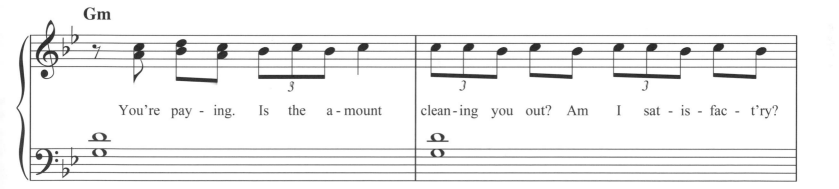

You're pay-ing. Is the a-mount clean-ing you out? Am I sat-is-fac-t'ry?

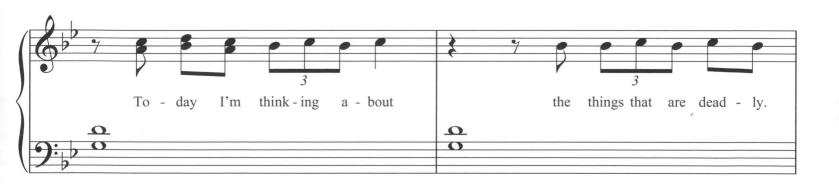

To-day I'm think-ing a-bout the things that are dead-ly.

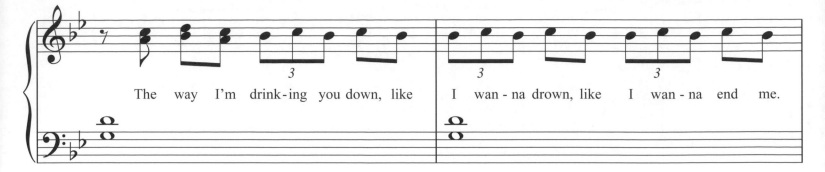

The way I'm drink-ing you down, like I wan-na drown, like I wan-na end me.

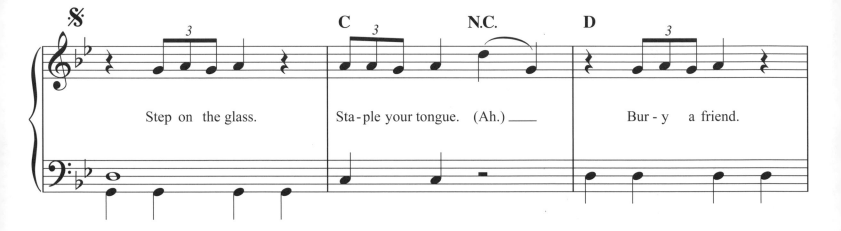

Step on the glass. Sta-ple your tongue. (Ah.) ____ Bur-y a friend.

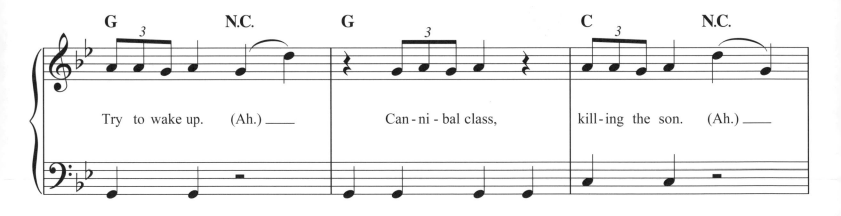

Try to wake up. (Ah.) ____ Can-ni-bal class, kill-ing the son. (Ah.) ____

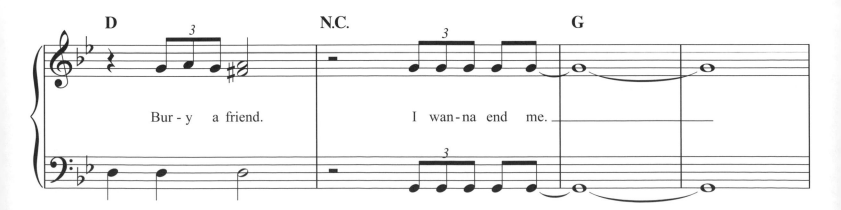

Bur-y a friend. I wan-na end me. ____

I wan-na end me. I wan-na, I wan-na,

I wan-na end me. I wan-na, I wan-na, I wan-na.

What do you want ___ from me? Why do you run ___ from me? What are you won - der-ing?

What do you know? ___ Why aren't you scared ___ of me? Why do you care ___ for me?

When we all fall _____ a - sleep, where do we go? _____

(Lis - ten.) Keep you in the dark. What had you ex - pect - ed:

me to make you my art and make you a star and get you con - nect - ed?

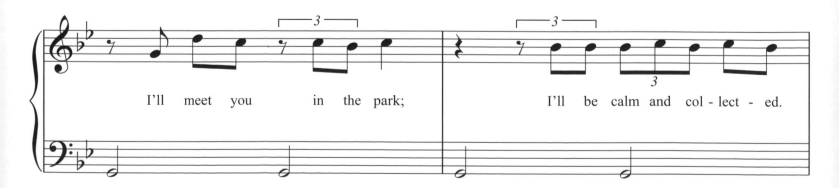

I'll meet you in the park; I'll be calm and col - lect - ed.

But we knew right from the start that you'd fall a-part, 'cause I'm too ex-pen-sive.

It's prob-a-bly some-thing that should-n't be said __ out __ loud.

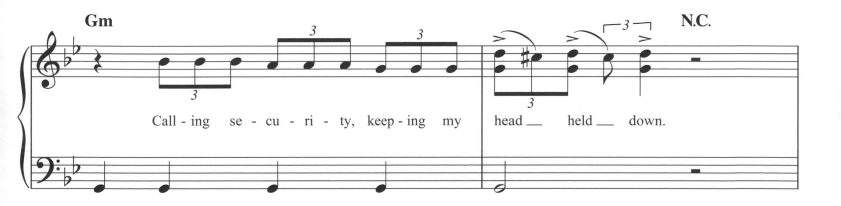

Hon-est-ly, I thought that I would be dead __ by __ now. (Wow.) __

Call-ing se-cu-ri-ty, keep-ing my head __ held __ down.

Bur-y the hatch-et or bur-y a friend right now. For the debt I owe, got-ta

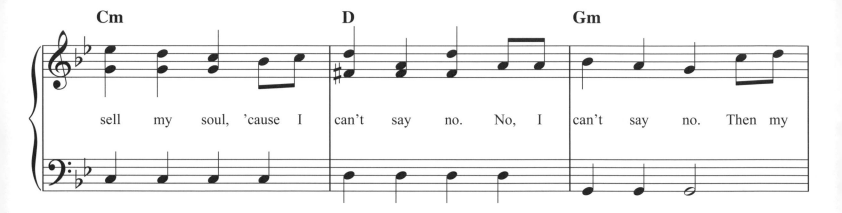

sell my soul, 'cause I can't say no. No, I can't say no. Then my

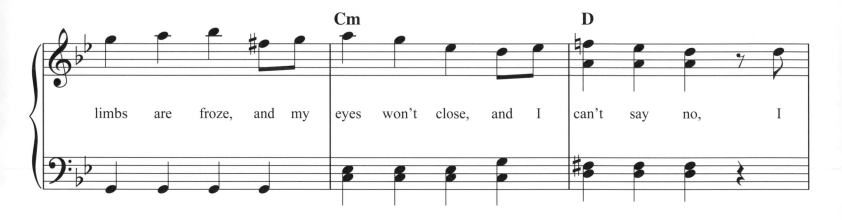

limbs are froze, and my eyes won't close, and I can't say no, I

can't say no. (Care-ful.)

When we all fall a-sleep, where do we go?

ilomilo

Words and Music by BILLIE EILISH O'CONNELL
and FINNEAS O'CONNELL

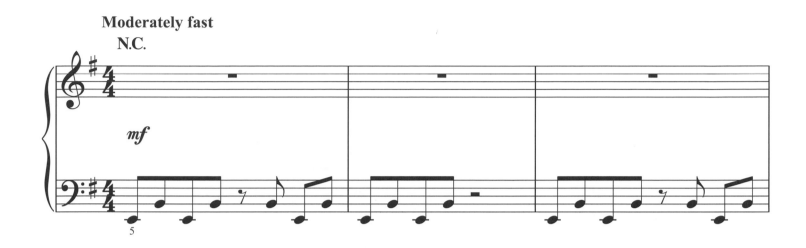

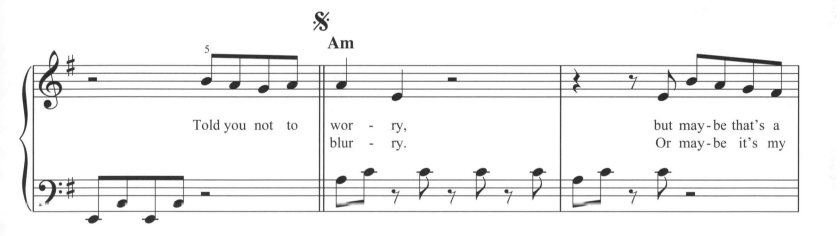

Won't you stay in - side?
They keep me up at night.

Re-mem - ber not to
Said I could-n't love some-

get   too close   to   start.   They're nev - er   gon - na   give   you love   like
one,   'cause I   to   might   break.   If you're gon - na   die,   not by   like mis -

ours. _____   Where did you   go? __   I should know, __   but it's cold __ and I   don't
take. _____   So   where did you   go? __   I should know, __   but it's   cold __ and I   don't

wan - na   be   lone - ly;   so   show ___   me the   way ___   home. _
wan - na   be   lone - ly;   so   tell ____   me   you'll   come _   home, _

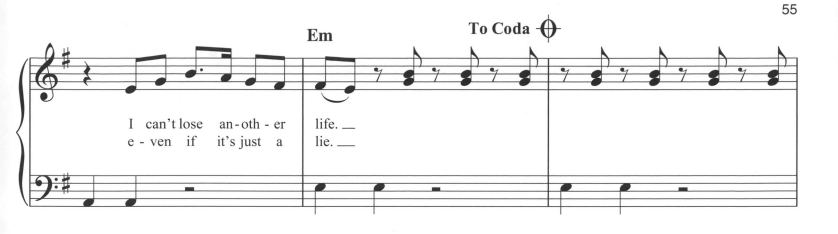

Em   To Coda ⊕

I can't lose an-oth-er life. __
e-ven if it's just a lie. __

Em11   Em   Bm7

Hur - ry.   I'm   wor -

Em/B   N.C.   D.S. al Coda

ried.   The world's a lit - tle

CODA ⊕

I tried not to up -

Bm

set you or let you   res - cue me. The day I   met you I just

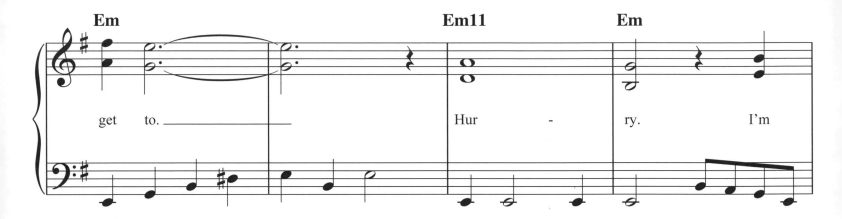

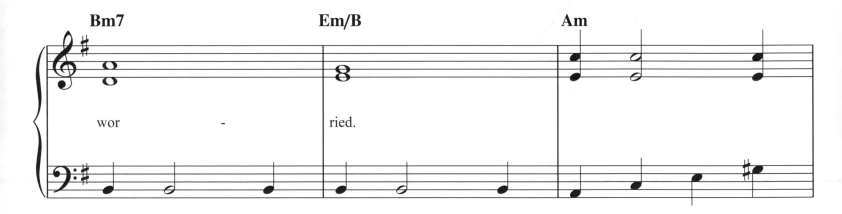

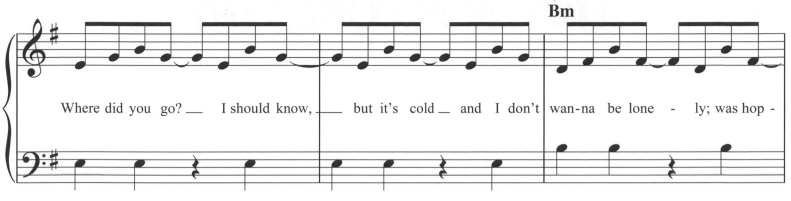

Where did you go? __ I should know, __ but it's cold __ and I don't wan-na be lone - ly; was hop -

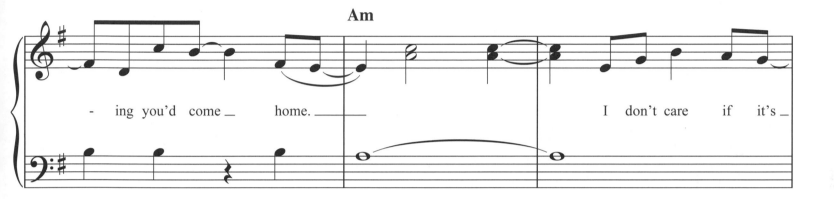

- ing you'd come __ home. _____ I don't care if it's _

_ a lie. _____

mp

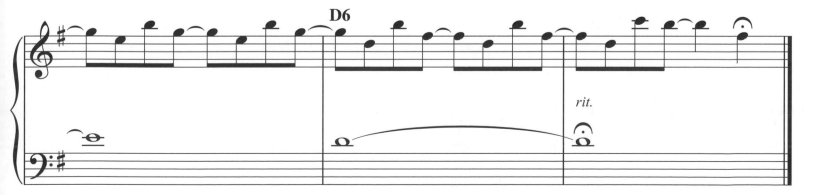

rit.

LISTEN BEFORE I GO

Words and Music by BILLIE EILISH O'CONNELL
and FINNEAS O'CONNELL

Very slowly, in 2

Take me to the roof - top. I wan - na see the

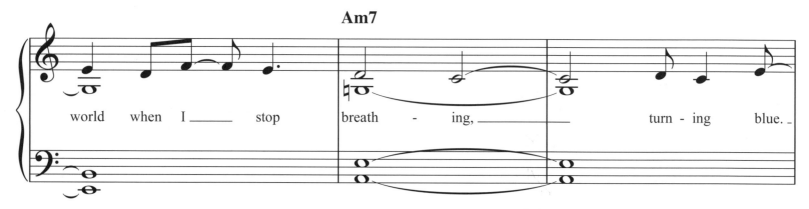

world when I ___ stop breath - ing, ___ turn - ing blue.

Tell me

love is end - less. Don't be so pre - ten - tious.

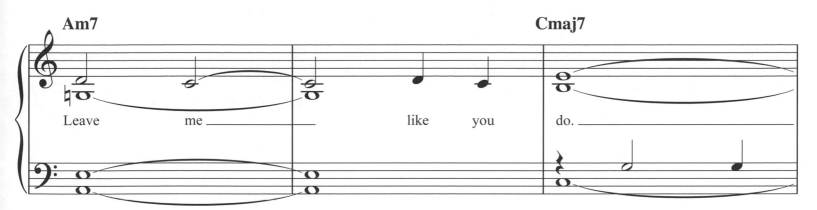

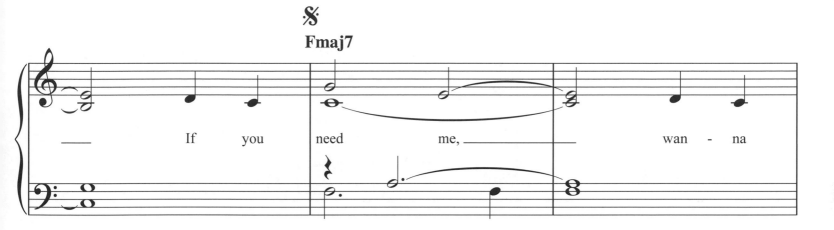

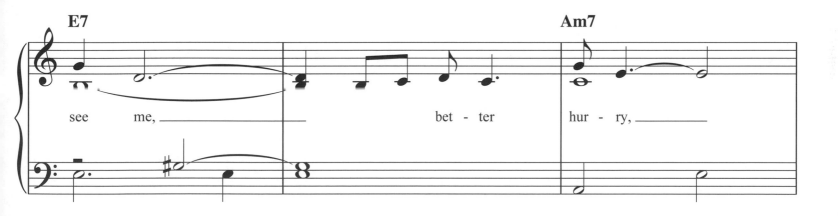

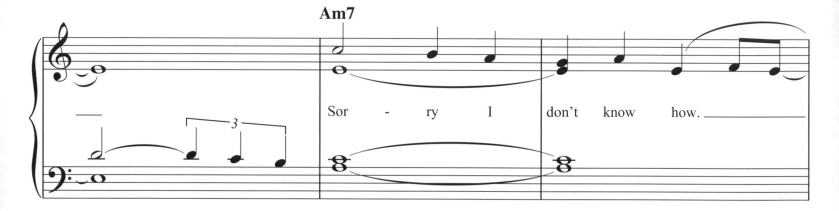

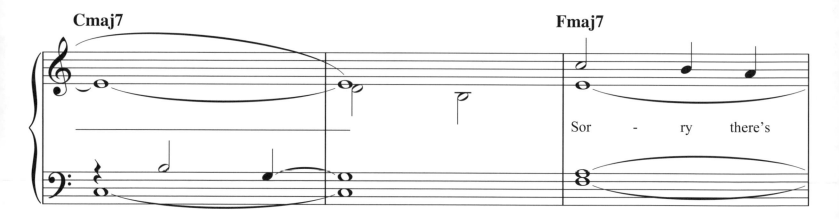

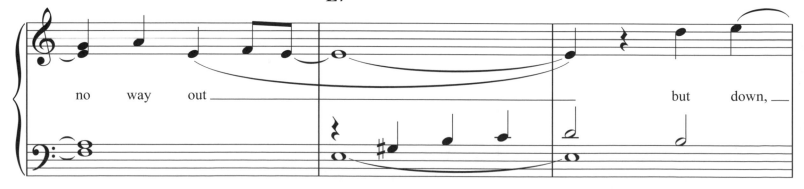

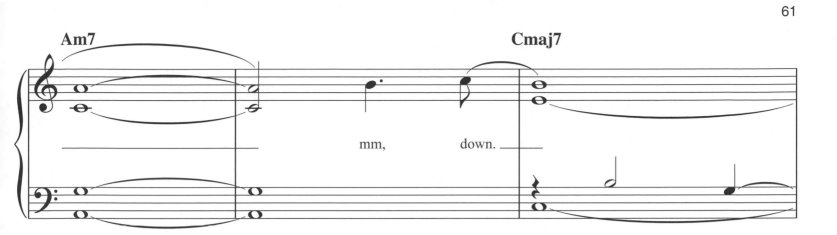

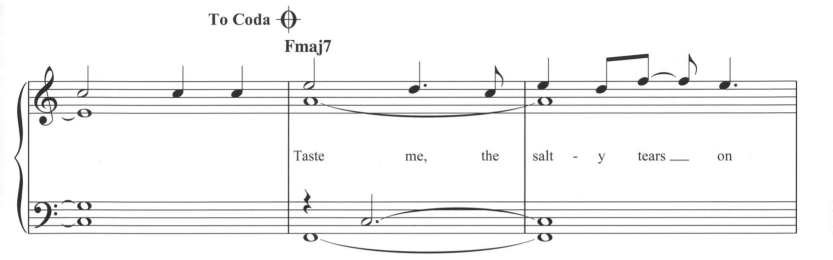

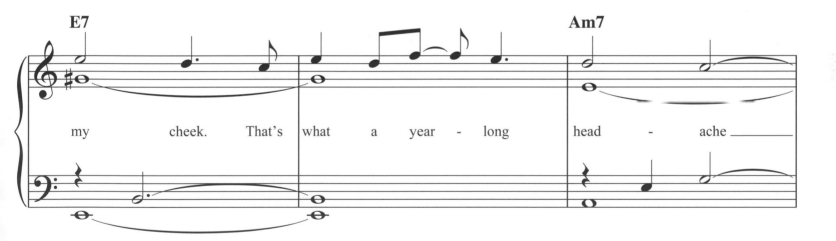

not o - kay, feel so scat - tered. Don't say I'm

all that mat - ters. Leave me. _____ Dé - jà vu. _____

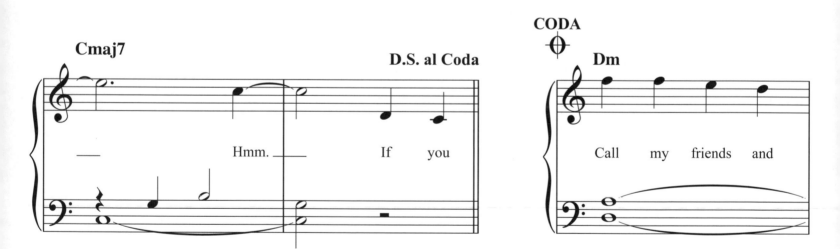

_____ Hmm. ____ If you

Call my friends and

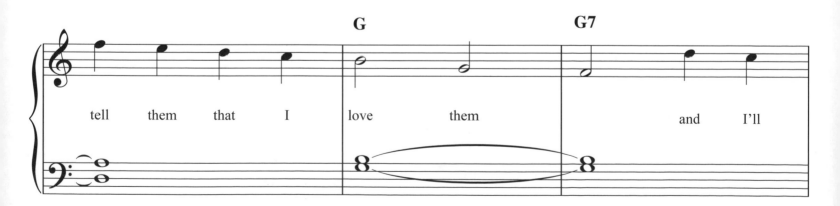

tell them that I love them and I'll

miss them, _____ _____ but I'm not sor - ry. _____

_____ Call my friends and tell them _____ that I _____

_____ love them _____ and I'll miss them. _____

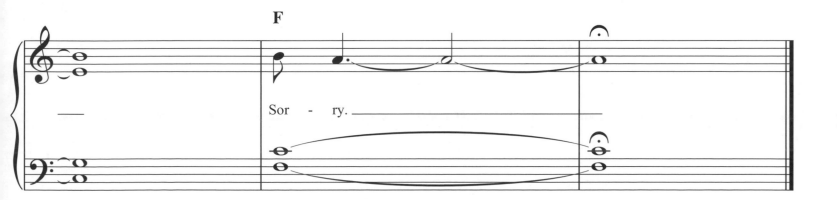

_____ Sor - ry. _____

I LOVE YOU

Words and Music by BILLIE EILISH O'CONNELL
and FINNEAS O'CONNELL

Moderately

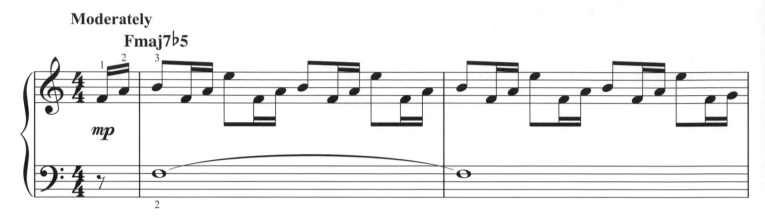

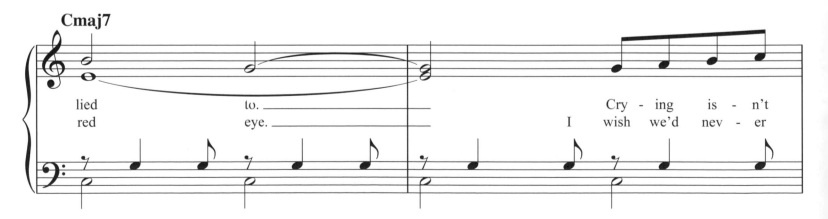

Fmaj7

like you. Ooh.
learned to fly. I.

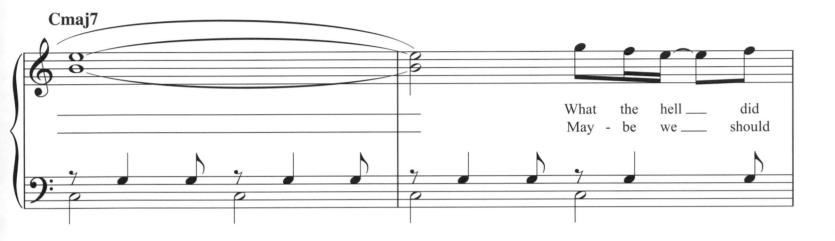

Cmaj7

What the hell did
May - be we should

Fmaj7

I do?
just try to tell our - selves a

Nev - er been the

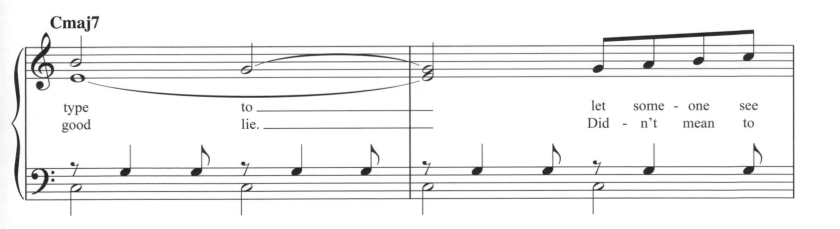

Cmaj7

type to let some - one see
good lie. Did - n't mean to

Fmaj7

right
make you cry, _____
through. _____
Ooh. _____
I. _____

Cmaj7

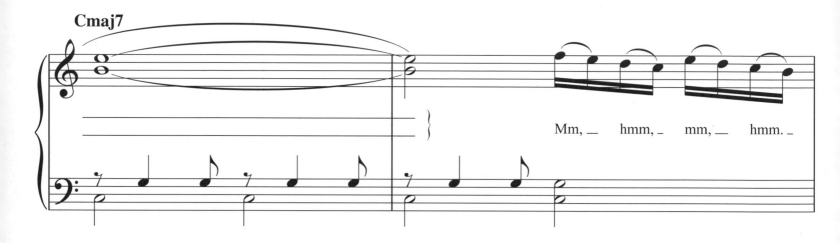

Mm, __ hmm, __ mm, __ hmm. __

F

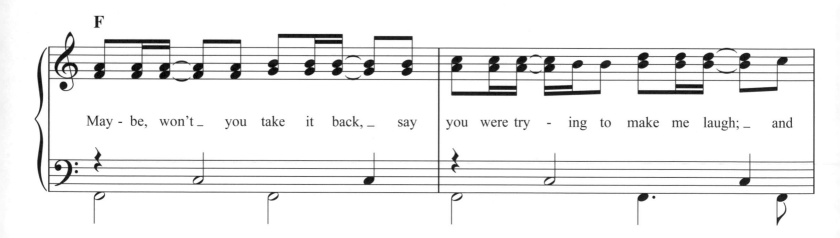

May - be, won't _ you take it back, _ say you were try - ing to make me laugh; _ and

G

noth - ing has _ to change to - day, _ you did - n't mean _ to say, "I love

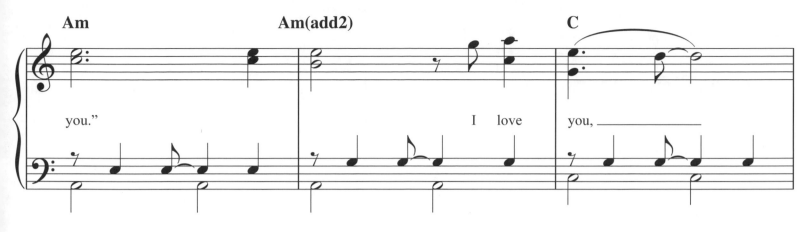

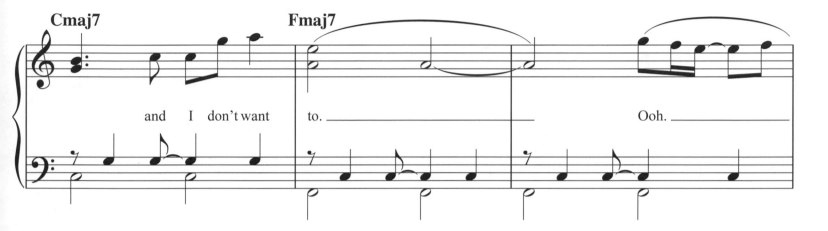

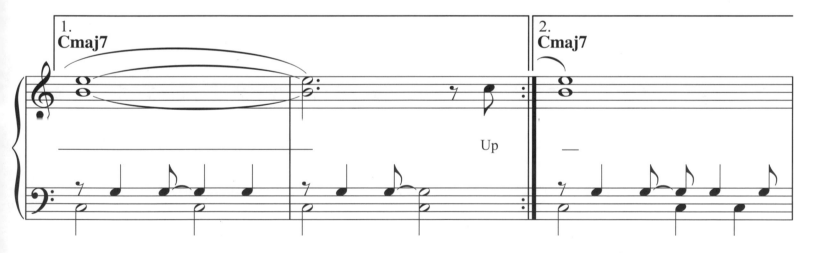

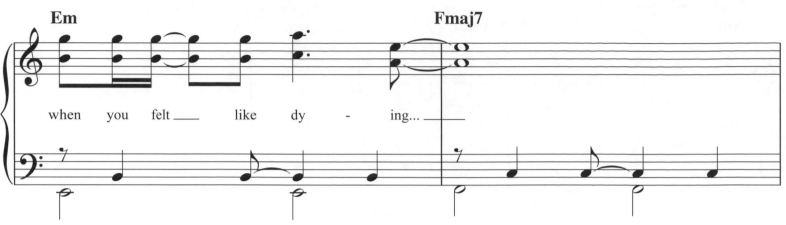

Em ... **Fmaj7**

when you felt ___ like dy - ing...

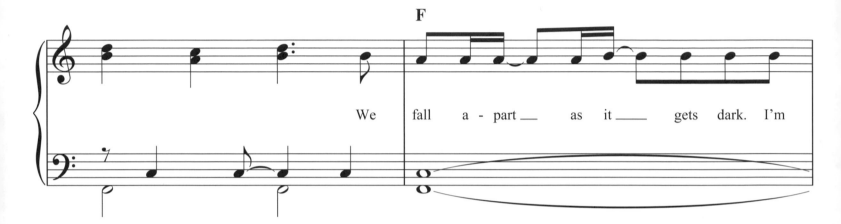

F

We fall a - part ___ as it ___ gets dark. I'm

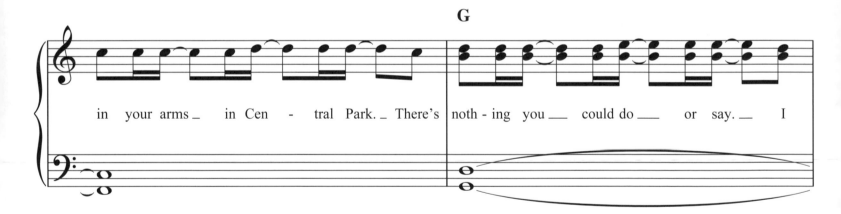

G

in your arms ___ in Cen - tral Park. ___ There's noth - ing you ___ could do ___ or say. ___ I

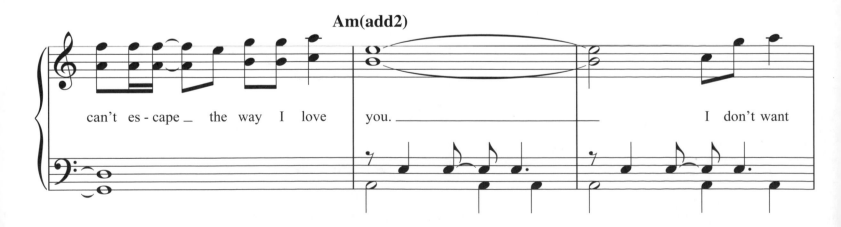

Am(add2)

can't es - cape ___ the way I love you. ___ I don't want

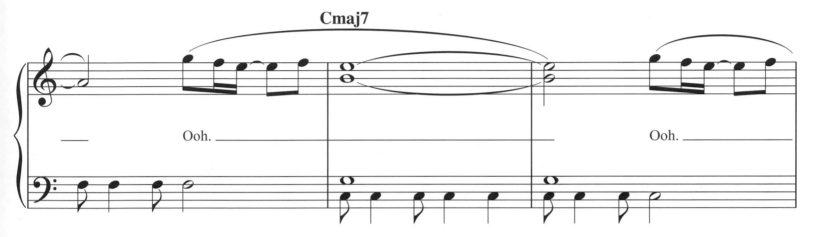

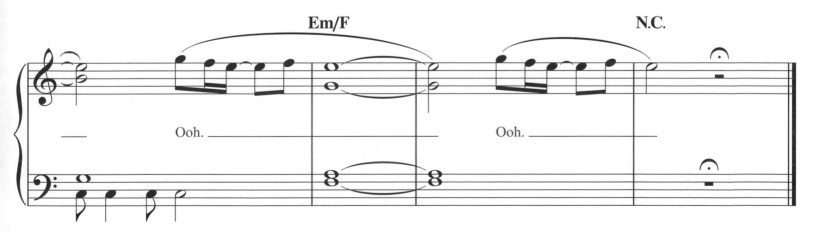

GOODBYE

Words and Music by BILLIE EILISH O'CONNELL
and FINNEAS O'CONNELL

Em · Eb+ · Gmaj7/D · C#m7b5 · Am

Don't ask ques-tions. _____ Wait a min - ute. Don't you know I'm no good for

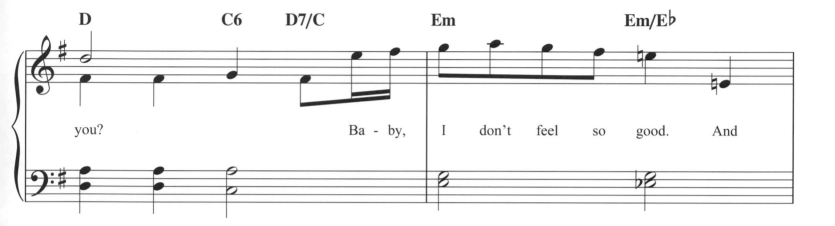

D · C6 · D7/C · Em · Em/Eb

you? Ba - by, I don't feel so good. And

Gmaj7/D · C#m7b5 · Am · D · D7/C

all the good girls go to hell. Bite my tongue, bide my time. What is it a-

Em · Eb+ · Gmaj7/D · C#m7b5 · Am

bout them? _____ *rit.* I'm the bad guy, ___ hmm.